Velociraptor

by Charles Lennie

ABDO
DINOSAURS
Kids

www.abdopublishing.com

Published by Abdo Kids, a division of ABDO, PO Box 398166, Minneapolis, Minnesota 55439.

Copyright © 2015 by Abdo Consulting Group, Inc. International copyrights reserved in all countries. No part of this book may be reproduced in any form without written permission from the publisher.

Printed in the United States of America, North Mankato, Minnesota.

052014

092014

Photo Credits: Alamy, AP Images, Getty Images, Shutterstock, Thinkstock, © Eric Kilby / Flickr.com Cover, © User: ho visto nina volare / CC-BY-SA-2.0 p. 7, © Salvatore Rabito Alcón / CC-BY-3.0 p.9, © User: Thesupermat / CC-BY-SA-3.0 p.21, © Thomas Cowart / CC-BY-2.0 p.21

Production Contributors: Teddy Borth, Jennie Forsberg, Grace Hansen

Design Contributors: Candice Keimig, Laura Rask, Dorothy Toth

Library of Congress Control Number: 2013952307

Cataloging-in-Publication Data

Lennie, Charles.

 Velociraptor / Charles Lennie.

  p. cm. -- (Dinosaurs)

ISBN 978-1-62970-027-4 (lib. bdg.)

Includes bibliographical references and index.

1. Velociraptor--Juvenile literature.   I. Title.

567.912--dc23

              2013952307

Table of Contents

Velociraptor

The Velociraptor lived a long time ago. It lived about 73 million years ago.

4

5

The Velociraptor was small. It was about the size of a turkey.

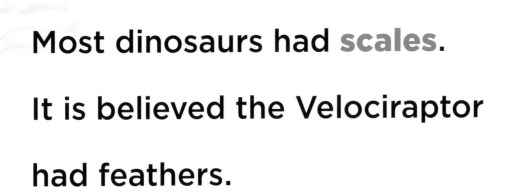

Most dinosaurs had **scales**.

It is believed the Velociraptor had feathers.

8

The Velociraptor had two very short arms. Each arm had three curved claws.

The Velociraptor had

two skinny legs.

12

The Velociraptor had a long tail. Its tail helped it to **balance** while it ran.

14

Hunting and Food

The Velociraptor had very

sharp teeth. Its teeth helped

it catch **prey**.

17

The Velociraptor ate meat. It probably ate small, slow dinosaurs.

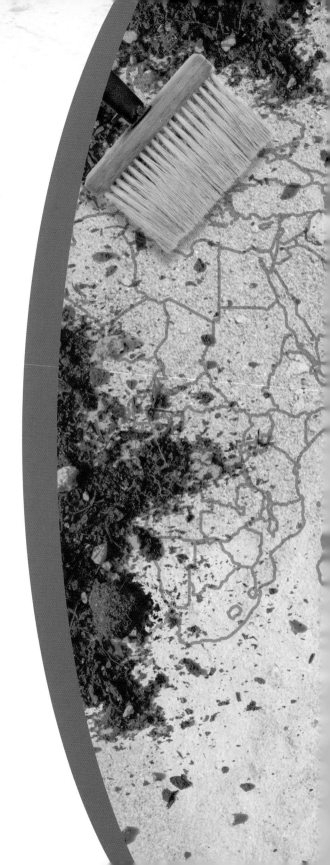

Fossils

Velociraptor **fossils** have been found in Mongolia. They have also been found in northern China.

Mongolia

China

More Facts

- The first known Velociraptor **fossil** was found in the Gobi desert in 1922.

- It was not until recently that scientists discovered the Velociraptor had feathers.

- The most famous dinosaur fossil ever found was a Velociraptor. It was in the middle of a battle with a Protoceratops.

- A Velociraptor's best defense and hunting tool were its long, sharp claws.

22

Glossary

balance – to keep from falling over.

fossil – the remains of a living thing;
could be a footprint or skeleton.

prey – an animal hunted or killed for food.

scales – flat plates that form the outer
covering of reptiles.

Index

abdokids.com

Use this code to log on to abdokids.com and access crafts, games, videos and more!

Abdo Kids Code:
DVK0274